W9-AVD-192

Promises Worth Keeping

Resolving to Live What We Say We Believe

A D U L T   J O U R N A L

Dedicated to those who have taken seriously
the challenge of being a Promise Keeper

CONTENTS

Accelerated Spiritual Growth
for Individuals and Families

This journal was created with input from more than 40 pastors and laypersons from across North America.

Writing team: Dr. David R. Mains (Director of The Chapel Ministries), Rev. Greg Asimakoupoulos, Brad Davis, Beth Johnson, Jennifer Knaak, Patric Knaak, Marian Oliver, Randy Petersen

Cover Illustration: Joe VanSeveren
Cover and Text Design: De Leon Design

The passion of Mainstay Church Resources is to facilitate revival among God's people by helping pastors help people develop healthy spiritual habits in nine vital areas that always characterize genuine times of spiritual awakening. To support this goal, Mainstay Church Resources uses a C.H.U.R.C.H. strategy to provide practical tools and resources including the annual 50-Day Spiritual Adventure, the Seasonal Advent Celebration, the 4-Week Festival of Worship, and the Pastor's Toolbox.

Printed in the United States of America
ISBN 1-57849-105-3

THE CHAPEL OF THE AIR MINISTRIES

MAINSTAY
Church Resources

**Helping Pastors
Help People Grow**

A revolution is sweeping the continent. Thousands of men have been packing stadiums throughout the land, voicing their unflagging commitment to a common goal. They're pushing a fundamental change in the way people live. They shout their vows in a deafening roar, pledging their very lives to this cause.

Scary stuff, huh?

It could be, except these men are promising to love their families, to support their churches, to serve their God. They're known as Promise Keepers, and our society has never seen anything quite like it. Who would have thought that over one million men would gather in Washington, D.C., in October 1997 to "Stand in the Gap"?

Of course, any movement has its foes, and people quickly filled newspaper columns and airwaves with their concerns. Chief among the questions was this: "What about women? Can't they keep promises too?"

Absolutely. It's just that many men admit to being, shall we say, "promise-challenged." Now God has seen to it that they've had this extra boost.

There's been another, quieter, revolution over the last two decades. The 50-Day Spiritual Adventure has been helping Christians to accelerate their spiritual growth. Through journals, books, and meaningful action steps, believers are making significant new strides in their Christian lives. Some have developed healthy spiritual habits of prayer and Bible reading. Some have restored relationships or broken destructive behavior patterns.

The Adventure has always been about taking challenges, making promises, and keeping them. With this new "PK" 50–Day Spiritual Adventure, everyone can learn to live what they say they believe. The same commitments that have energized stadiums full of men can breathe new life into entire families and congregations.

So strap yourself in and get ready to fly. This Adventure may well change your life. You'll be making promises that will improve your relationships, and you'll be counting on God's power to stay true to them. There are seven themes that correspond to the seven Promise Keepers promises. The eighth theme encourages us to live every day through Christ's resurrection power.

With God's help, I promise to:

1. Nurture a growing intimacy with the Lord Jesus Christ.
2. Cultivate vital friendships that encourage me to keep my promises.
3. Practice purity in thought and action.
4. Make family relationships a priority.
5. Support the ministry of my church and pastor.
6. Identify and address the hidden prejudices of my heart.
7. Influence my world with the love of Christ.
8. Live one day at a time through the power of the risen Christ.

How Can This Journal Change My Life?

This is more than an ordinary Bible study you're holding. It's a road map to accelerated spiritual growth—a Spiritual Adventure that can change your life. We trust that two months from now, as you've allowed God's Spirit to work in your life, you will be a stronger and more authentic Christian.

After finishing the Adventure, you should have established at least one new, healthy spiritual habit. If you can accomplish that in one strategic area of your spiritual life, you will have made enormous progress forward. And that's what this Adventure is all about: accelerating our spiritual growth, making spiritual progress, and developing our relationship with the Lord. So make it your personal goal to establish at least one new, healthy spiritual habit.

Nearly one million people will be going on this Spiritual Adventure with you. Tens of thousands of churches will benefit as the Lord touches individual lives like yours. It will be a time of growth for everyone involved. All of that starts as you turn these pages and intentionally begin to study the Scriptures, pray, and put into practice the action steps in this journal. There's a lot going on here, but don't be overwhelmed. Just take the Adventure one day at a time, and you'll be fine.

What do I need in order to do the 50-Day Spiritual Adventure successfully?

1. *Your Bible.* Regular Scripture reading is an important part of this Adventure. Each day we suggest a passage of Scripture that coordinates with the weekly theme. Make sure you're using a Bible you understand.

2. *This journal.* Here is where you'll be processing what you're reading each day. We offer a few questions to help you get at the meaning of the text and how it applies to your life. This journal is not an intensive Bible study guide; it's primarily a tool for life application. Along with the daily Scripture questions, you'll find instructions for action steps that will aid you in living out the biblical principles you're learning.

3. *The Audio Guidebook*—*People of Promise: How to Be an Authentic Believer* by J. Daniel Lupton. This inspiring audio-book will help you incorporate the eight themes of the Adventure into your life. The author's personal stories and insightful illustrations will challenge you to keep your promises with God's help. Listen to a chapter a week to keep current. (See p. 20 for ordering information.)

4. *A good attitude.* This Adventure will stretch you if you're open to spiritual growth. Take it seriously, but not *too* seriously! Don't let it load you with guilt, and don't carry into the Adventure a negative disposition. Instead, have fun with the Adventure, and let God work within you to develop some healthy new spiritual habits.

What do I have to do?

There are assignments for you to complete each day of the Adventure. First, you'll need to read the suggested Scripture passage and answer the questions in the journal. We also recommend that you choose some Bible verses to memorize. One per week is a good goal to shoot for. *The Little Scripture Pack for Practicing Purity*, duplicated on pages 121–126, contains 22 verses for you to choose from.

Second, you will want to listen to a chapter every week in the resourceful Audio Guidebook, *People of Promise: How to Be an Authentic Believer.* And then there are the important action steps. . . .

Why are these action steps so powerful?
The action steps are specific activities we're suggesting you do to begin living out these seven promises. The steps are practical, proven ways to help you apply the Word of God to your everyday life. The next few pages will explain them thoroughly. The first action step asks you to create weekly memorable moments with Jesus. The second encourages you to come out of spiritual isolation. The third helps you confess and confront a signature sin. Next, you find simple ways to care for those you care about. Finally, the fifth action step asks you to choose to become exposed to the suffering of others.

The Adventure works well when you follow our suggestions, but you may choose to customize them to fit your situation. If one of the action steps is driving you crazy, forget it and focus on the others. (For a quick overview of all the Adventure assignments, see p. 20.)

How much time is involved?
We estimate it will take just 10–15 minutes per day to complete the daily journal assignments. Listening to the Audio Guidebook will require an extra half hour per week. And you'll need a few additional time blocks during the 50-day period to complete some action steps.

Does that sound like too much? We hope not. As with any important relationship, it's hard to grow closer to Christ if you don't devote priority time to him each day.

How do I keep track of everything?
We will prompt you throughout this journal with check boxes to help you keep current with the action steps. For a quick overview of where you've been and where you're headed each week, see the "Looking Back . . . Moving Forward" pages, usually after each Friday journal page. If your church is doing the Adventure and you're being asked to join in on the Congregational Affirmation each week, you will need to decide each Friday whether you want to participate.

Do I need to follow the journal every day?
Yes. But if you miss a day or two, don't panic! It's best to pick up the journal entries with the current day, rather than try to make up those you've skipped.

What's different about Saturday/Sunday pages?
Each of the eight themes is introduced with a format different from the other journal pages. On weekends, a commentary by Dr. David Mains sets the tone for the days that follow.

Can I Adventure with my friends or family?
Absolutely. That's a great way to make it even more meaningful. This will take some extra time as you discuss the scriptures or review one another's progress on the action steps, but the mutual accountability and encouragement will be of great benefit. And we provide lots of help with journals for adults, students, and children, along with small group materials. While not a large print resource, the pamphlet *Adventuring with Friends and Family* may give you some ideas. It is available through your church or by calling Mainstay Church Resources at 1-800-224-2735.

What if I want a more in-depth approach to the Adventure?
On each "Looking Back . . . Moving Forward" page, you'll find optional follow-up Scriptures for further reading on the topic of the week.

What can I do to keep going when the Adventure is over?
Once you've finished the Adventure, you will undoubtedly want to continue with several of the spiritual habits you've developed over these 50 days. One suggestion is to simply repeat this Adventure by getting another journal to write in.

Can I follow the Adventure on radio?
You bet. Many participants will benefit from the two-minute "Spiritual Adventure" carried on numerous radio stations throughout North America. To find out when and where to tune in, call Mainstay Church Resources at 1-800-224-2735.

Where should I start?
Familiarize yourself with the five action steps on pages 8–19. You might also flip through the day-to-day section of the journal starting on page 24. Then, to give yourself a head start on the Friday before Day 1, begin the Warm-up Day exercises on pages 21–22.

ONE

Create Memorable Moments with Jesus

Your house is on fire. You only have time to rescue one armload of possessions from the flames. Your family and pets have already scampered to safety. It's just you and your stuff. What's most precious to you?

Most people would pass by the expensive objects in their homes; those items can be replaced by the insurance claim. Instead, they'd grab the photo album, the correspondence drawer, Brad's school papers, the afghan that dear Aunt Edna knitted before she passed away. These items can't be replaced, because they hold memorable moments from the past.

The strongest families and friendships have lots of great moments tucked away, in photo albums or just in people's memories. "Remember when . . . ?" Some can talk for hours about the precious times they've shared with those closest to them.

Does your relationship with Christ have memorable moments like that? Perhaps the time you first met him? Or the moment you first felt the Bible was speaking to you? But have there been many moments like that lately?

Any relationship is in trouble when all its memorable moments are ancient history. Friends and families need to keep creating new occasions of love and caring, of growth and fun. That's how relationships grow. Of course, the same is true with Jesus. Have you created any memorable moments with him recently? Maybe it's time to put some new pictures in that photo album.

Instructions

Set aside 15 minutes or more each week for a special time with Jesus, an opportunity to create memorable moments in your relationship together. Ask, "What would you want me to do, Jesus, if I were to give you 15 uninterrupted minutes each of these seven Adventure weeks?" Here are some ideas others have tried:

Things You Might Do to Create Memorable Moments with Jesus

- Get rid of all distractions and listen to a favorite Christian CD or tape. Sing along, if it seems appropriate.
- Enjoy his handiwork. Walk in a flower garden. Take a short hike in the outdoors and marvel at God's creative genius. If you have the time, visit a zoo or a planetarium.
- Sit in silence and tell God that you want to make your mind and heart sensitive to any messages he might have for you.
- Check out a library book of religious paintings and browse through it. Try to picture yourself in the scenes you find most interesting.
- Choose a helpful verse from *The Little Scripture Pack for Practicing Purity*, duplicated on pages 121–126. Memorize it so it will be yours the next time you are tempted.
- Write a poem, compose a song, or create something with your hands, and offer it in praise to the Lord.

The bottom line is to fashion seven memorable moments that you can look back at with great satisfaction. These, along with journaling and daily use of the following prayer, will help you nurture a growing intimacy with the Lord.

The Promises Worth Keeping Prayer

Lord, I want a growing relationship with you. I'm tired of broken promises. Guide me to godly friends who will help me remain pure and honor my priorities. Open my eyes to hidden prejudices in my life. Open my heart to the needs of my church and its leaders. Teach me to reflect your love in the world around me. Help me to _____ so I can live today what I say I believe. Amen.

ACTION STEP

Come Out of Spiritual Isolation

Every week, before and after worship services, churches are packed with Christians talking. But what are they talking about?

"What's happening at work?"

"How 'bout those Packers?"

"That's a beautiful sweater. Where'd you get it?"

"Was *Home Improvement* good this week?"

Nothing wrong with those subjects, but why don't Christians talk more about *Christ?* Just imagine what would happen if you started saying things like:

"Update me on that issue you requested prayer for last month."

"What pressures or temptations are you facing right now?"

"Have you been keeping up on the Adventure action steps?"

"What did you do during your special 15 minutes with Jesus this week?"

Sure, some people would look at you like your hair was on fire, but others would open up to you—and your friendship would find a whole new vitality that would benefit you both.

We don't ask about people's spiritual lives because we don't want to offend them. That's *personal stuff*, we assume—but this results in a kind of spiritual isolation, with each of us closely guarding the details of our Christian growth.

Shouldn't Christian friendships be able to cross that line? We need to give one another permission to ask about spiritual things. Too often we follow a "don't ask, don't tell" policy about our Christian experience. Let's start asking, and let's start telling. We need to cultivate vital friendships with people who can help us grow closer to Christ and keep our promises.

Instructions

Ask a friend or family member to touch base with you each week of the Adventure. If you don't have someone specific in mind, pray that the Lord will lead you to the right person. This could even result in a long-term relationship. This person will simply ask how you're doing on the promises and on the action steps. (See below for a few other question ideas.) If your friend is also on the Adventure, you could be partners, checking up on each other. And you could easily add a third or fourth person to the partnership, as long as you're all spending time sharing your progress on the Adventure. This might also be a good time to consider getting a small group started, which will facilitate even more sharing and interaction.

Questions to Ask One Another
- What simple act of servant love has someone done for you? (See Action Step 4.)
- What have you learned about Jesus during your special 15 minutes with him? (See Action Step 1.)
- How are you doing on the daily Scripture studies?
- Which action step are you finding most difficult?
- How can I help you keep your promises?
- How can I be praying for you?

Tips for the Adventure Checkup
- Be honest. This is no time to prove how spiritual you are. If you're having trouble, say so.
- You're allowed to say, "No comment." If a question feels threatening to you, skip it.
- If you're asking the questions, don't pry. Allow the other person some privacy.
- You may fail at some things during this Adventure. If so, just pick up and keep going. No guilt trips, but don't give up either.

ACTION STEP

THREE

Confess and Confront a Signature Sin

Try not to think of a four-letter word.

Did a bad one already come to mind?

Well, don't think about any others. Don't count the letters on your fingers as you spell another word that pops into your head.

Hey, that's the problem with purity. You want to get rid of a problem sin and stay clean, so you concentrate on abolishing that sin, and then you start focusing on that sin, and soon it's hard to stop thinking about that sin, and then it's next to impossible to stop committing it.

That's in spite of the fact that sin makes promises it can't keep. Sexual sin promises fulfillment. Pride promises satisfaction. Cheating promises advancement. But all those promises are ultimately broken.

Purity means selling out totally to the God who keeps every promise. Why not exchange your problem sin for a new way of living, close beside your trustworthy Lord?

Instructions

In this action step, you'll be identifying one area of impurity in your life and trusting God's power to defeat it. You'll begin this process in Adventure Week 3. To help you, we've created an acronym for PURITY.

• **Put your name by a signature sin.** That is, identify a recurring temptation you struggle with. Mentally initial that sin that could be your nickname. (For example, "Liar," "Workaholic," "Prideful," or "Foul Mouth.") A signature sin is that sin you "own" (or, in reality, it "owns" you). Like a loan document, it's a temptation that boasts of your signature at the bottom of the page. And because you've signed your name, as that temptation demands payment, you regularly comply. In order to move toward purity, you need to learn how to start skipping payments. But begin by coming to terms with your "debt."

• **Unmask who you are before God.** Once you've owned your signature sin, you're in a position to admit to the Lord what he's known all along. The Bible calls that kind of candid honesty "confession." Quit playing the game of "I'm OK, you're OK" with God. Bare your soul before him. Genuinely express how much you want to quit being known as a gossip or cheat or as someone addicted to pornography or alcohol. Share your hope of being healed, but also confess your fear of failure. You may hesitate taking steps toward purity because of the number of times you have tried and tripped. But God knows your track record. He can handle your honest doubt.

• **Replace old patterns with new possibilities.** Chances are, you've shaped your life around your signature sin. Getting rid of it will involve changing patterns in order to avoid temptation and refocus on positive thoughts or activities. If lust is a problem, you need to break the cycle that routinely results in dirty thoughts. Stop doing what you always do. Ask God how he feels about your fantasies or viewing habits. Destroy the books, videos, and magazines you've stashed away. Gather the courage to cancel your subscription to cable channels or periodicals you'd be ashamed to look at with Jesus. For the remainder of the Adventure, promise yourself (and the Lord) that you will not knowingly look at what trips the land mine of lust in your mind.

If you struggle with envy, determine not to look at fashion or decorating magazines that cause you to covet. Enter willingly into a "shopping fast." Break the cycle. Picture the possibility of a more contented "you." Create a new picture of yourself. On one side of a page list words that describe you when you give in to your signature sin. Do you want to be defined by them? When you lose your temper, are you happy with yourself? How about when you deceive someone? Now move to the other side of the page. List five words or phrases that picture a different you. How much do you long to be a new person? Ask God to give you eyes to see what his unconditional love makes possible.

• **Identify Scriptures that keep you focused.** When confronted with temptation, the first ten seconds are crucial. So why not be prepared? Jesus was. When he faced Satan in the wilderness, he immediately spoke out the Word of God he'd hidden in his heart. You can too.

Memorize certain Bible verses that arm you against the garden variety of sins that keep sprouting in your head. When you're tempted to complain and grumble, instantly blurt out, "May the words of my mouth and the thoughts of my heart be pleasing to you, O Lord, my rock and my redeemer" (Psalm 19:14). *The Little Scripture Pack for Practicing Purity,* (duplicated on pp. 121–126.) will come in handy.

• **Trust a friend to help you.** We need each other to help us get through our struggles and stay on course. Take Action Step 2 seriously. Have you identified a fellow adventurer yet? If you're in a small group, it could be one of the members. Whoever you choose, ask that person to call you once a week to see how you're doing. Share your struggles and victories confidentially. As you find yourself facing temptation, you may want to call that person. Ideally, you can be helping him or her as well. It can work both ways.

• **Yell for joy whenever you get it right.** You *can* find victory over this signature sin. Don't expect a gold medal tomorrow. The process may be lifelong, but there can be short-range victories one day at a time. As you say no to sin, learn how to celebrate your steps of progress. Talk to yourself. "Lord, with your help, I resisted what normally trips me up. Thanks! Do you feel as good about this as I do? I mean, we did it—yes-s-s-s!" Others may not be aware of your secret battle, so they won't be inclined to pat you on the back when you succeed. Affirm yourself. But don't despair when you fail. Instead, accept and celebrate God's forgiveness.

The phrase signature sin *was developed by Michael W. Mangis, associate professor of psychology at the Wheaton College Graduate School in Wheaton, Illinois.*

ACTION STEP

FOUR

Care for Those You Care About

"Luv ya, hon. Bye." "Later, Mom." "There's my ride. Gotta go."

In our hectic world, we often find ourselves running all over the place for work and other obligations—and even for our recreation. Sarah's off to violin lessons, Jonathan's at soccer practice, Mom's working late, and Dad's at a church board meeting. Even the best families seem to wave at each other as they pass.

That's often true of our friendships as well. We end up playing phone tag with our closest friends because there's just so much to do. Who has time for *people* anymore, even the people we care about most?

Obviously, there's something wrong with this picture. Every friendship is a promise, and family relationships are even more so. "I will be there for you; I will care for you; we'll have fun together." When we run right past one another, we're neglecting those promises.

Let's start turning that around. Let's *make* time and opportunities to care for one another.

Instructions

Every day of the Adventure, do something simple to care for someone you care about.

Start by identifying the people around you who need your caring touch. Perhaps you've neglected family members who should be the ones closest to you. If you're short on family, reach out to your circle of friends. Pastors and church leaders are often overlooked and under-encouraged. Be sure that some of your caring acts are directed toward them. Ask God to steer you toward the people he wants you to care for. Then log your activity on pages 64–65 of this journal.

Look for opportunities to serve. Do one simple act of servant love each day. It doesn't have to be a big production number. Do a chore normally reserved for a spouse or child. Make the bed. Drop a love note in a lunch box. Send an encouraging e-mail message. Give flowers. Take out the garbage. Make a phone call. Take someone out to dinner. Play street hockey with your kids—or your neighbors' kids. Give a hand massage. Take care of elderly parents. Encourage a coworker.

This action step won't take a lot of time; on many days your simple act will be spontaneous. But you'll probably want to plan ahead for some of your expressions of servant love. Planning and effort show we care.

A Letter from Coach McCartney

Dear Friend:

When God sends revival, I believe it will touch all churches and denominations across our nation in a powerful way. I pray that day will come soon.

We have already seen wonderful evidences that almighty God wants to do something special in our land. Along with many others the Lord is using, through our conferences and events like Stand in the Gap, our mass gathering of men in Washington, D.C., Promise Keepers has been privileged to help fan the flames of revival. I believe this 50-Day Spiritual Adventure, which is based on the Seven Promises of a Promise Keeper, will have a similar effect on congregations everywhere.

I'm thankful that you've chosen to be part of this exciting Adventure and to join the great team of Christian men and women who have resolved to live out what they say they believe in our time. God bless you!

Your servant,
Bill McCartney

The Seven Promises of a Promise Keeper

1. A Promise Keeper is committed to honor Jesus Christ through worship, prayer, and obedience to God's Word through the power of the Holy Spirit.

2. A Promise Keeper is committed to pursue vital relationships with a few other men, understanding that he needs brothers to help him keep his promises.

3. A Promise Keeper is committed to practice spiritual, moral, ethical, and sexual purity.

4. A Promise Keeper is committed to build a strong marriage and family through love, protection, and biblical values.

5. A Promise Keeper is committed to support the mission of his church by honoring and praying for his pastor and by actively giving his time and resources.

6. A Promise Keeper is committed to reach beyond any racial and denominational barriers to demonstrate the power of biblical unity.

7. A Promise Keeper is committed to influence his world, being obedient to the Great Commandment (see Mark 12:30–31) and the Great Commission (see Matthew 28:19–20).

ACTION STEP

FIVE

Choose to Become
Exposed to the Suffering of Others

Her name is Liberty. She has stood in New York harbor holding a torch for over one hundred years. Her silent stance shouts to other nations across the sea: "Give me your tired, your poor, your huddled masses yearning to breathe free. . . ." Millions have sailed beneath her outstretched arm to find freedom and opportunity in the United States.

America has long prided itself on being a melting pot of cultures and peoples. Canada also boasts a smorgasbord of ethnic diversity. This diversity extends to other areas. The rich, poor, and middle class. The athletic and the disabled. The employed and those on assistance. The retired and the young. Married and single. Parents and the childless. The homosexual. The alcoholic. The homeless.

It is one thing to acknowledge with pride that all people are promised life, liberty, and the pursuit of happiness under the law. But, it is another thing alto-

gether to reach out with understanding, compassion, and friendship to those who are different from us. If we are honest with ourselves, we would have to admit that we sometimes nurture hidden prejudices in our hearts that are inconsistent with our faith.

The inscription on the Statue of Liberty echoes the words of a rabbi who claimed to be the Light of the World. Jesus said, "Come unto me, *all* you who labor and are heavy-laden, and I will give you rest." The one we claim to follow connected with all kinds of people without prejudging them. He calls us to identify and address attitudes that prevent us from providing his grace to others.

Identifying and addressing what hides in our hearts begins with being aware of our attitudes to those around us. Next time you're stopped at a red light and you reach to lock your door, ask yourself why. Are you aware of the fact that you drive out of your way to get to a favorite store to avoid driving through a certain part of town? What about that rush of resentment you feel when all the parking slots in front of a fast-food restaurant are designated for the handicapped? Do you even think twice before declining an invitation to attend a benefit for those suffering from AIDS?

Once we are aware of our judgmental attitudes, we can bring ourselves to confess them and seek forgiveness. Perhaps then we can begin connecting with the plight of people unlike us, as Jesus did.

Instructions

Once during the Adventure, find a way to become exposed to the suffering of others. You might seek to address racial, ethnic, religious, gender, or economic barriers.

See a film or play that depicts the experience of a group you've been avoiding. *Amistad* will grip you as it talks about slavery. *Bury My Heart at Wounded Knee* provides a perspective on Native Americans. The VeggieTales *Are You My Neighbor?* challenges people of all ages. Karen Mains's book *Comforting One Another* shows how to extend mercy to those who are suffering. Host a meal and invite those of different groups you might not normally spend time with. Find a way to talk kindly to someone with AIDS or an individual hooked on drugs about the pain of their experiences. Reach out much like Christ did to those thought of as unclean during his time on earth. Consider asking any missionaries you know for help (most have had to deal with cross-cultural relationships). If you've never visited a nursing home, a mental institution, or ministered in a jail, here's your chance. Don't avoid the pain by avoiding the situation.

Whatever activity you choose, try to put yourself in the shoes of those on the other side of that barrier. Look at life from their perspective. Ask God to change your heart, according to what you learn.

You may find that the one-time activity of this Adventure will be the first of many. Perhaps you'll start building relationships across these barriers that will continue for many years. In that way, you'll be honoring the promise to identify and address hidden prejudices.

For a full description of the action steps, see pages 8–19. This journal will give you daily reminders and weekly checkups to guide you through the assignments.

DAILY

1. Study the assigned Scripture passages and answer the questions in the journal.
2. Pray the Promises Worth Keeping Prayer, using the model on page 9.
3. On the chart on pages 64–65, list your simple act of servant love.

WEEKLY

1. Listen to the appropriate chapter in the Audio Guidebook *People of Promise: How to Be an Authentic Believer.*
2. Set aside at least 15 minutes for a special time with Jesus, an opportunity to create memorable moments in your relationship together.
3. Memorize a Bible verse to help you confess and confront a signature sin.
4. Have a friend or family member ask you how you're doing on the promises and action steps.

ONCE DURING THE ADVENTURE

1. Identify a "signature sin," and trust God's power to defeat it.
2. Find a way to become exposed to the suffering of others.

A Necessary Resource for This 50-Day Adventure
People of Promise: How to Be an Authentic Believer
by J. Daniel Lupton (Audio Guidebook)

In addition to your Bible and journal, you need one copy of the Audio Guidebook. Filled with personal stories and practical illustrations, *People of Promise* provides an extra boost of support during the Adventure to help you keep your promises. This audiobook will enhance your 50-Day experience. Order the Audio Guidebook through your church or call Mainstay Church Resources at 1-800-224-2735.

WARM-UP

Promises Worth Keeping

Read 2 Peter 1:3—9.   **Date_____**

1. How would you describe the tone of this passage? What is Peter trying to encourage his readers to do?

_____

_____

2. According to verse 3, what is available to all believers?

_____

_____

3. In verse 4, Peter talks about "great and precious promises." What are some examples (e.g., Proverbs 3:5—6)?

_____

_____

4. What does Peter say are the benefits of applying his instructions? What are the consequences of failing to do so?

_____

_____

5. What benefits are you hoping to receive during the next 50 days?

_____

_____

_____

❏ Read the introductory material on pages 3—7.
❏ Pray the Promises Worth Keeping Prayer on page 9.
❏ Listen to the introduction in the Audio Guidebook, *People of Promise.* (see p. 20).

Promises Worth Keeping

Read John 15:1–17.   Date_____

1. In this passage, Jesus is speaking to his disciples for the last time before his arrest and crucifixion. What is his message regarding their relationship with him? What about their relationship with each other?

_____

_____

2. Jesus says repeatedly, "Remain in me." What do you think he means?

_____

_____

3. What are some of the results of remaining in Jesus? (See verses 2, 4–8, 11, 16.)

_____

_____

4. According to verses 14–15, what does Jesus call us if we obey his commands? Can you picture him calling you that? If so, describe how that makes you feel.

_____

_____

5. In what specific areas might Jesus desire to have more intimacy with you? What steps can you take to respond to his desires?

_____

_____

❑ Read the action step descriptions on pages 8–18.
❑ Pray the Promises Worth Keeping Prayer on page 9.
❑ Listen to the introduction in the Audio Guidebook, *People of Promise* (see p. 20).

Check the box if you have completed the assignment.

❑ Read the introductory materials on pages 3–7.

❑ Listened to the introduction in the Audio Guidebook, *People of Promise*.

❑ Completed the Warm-up Days on pages 21–22.

MOVING FORWARD

Theme 1: Nurture a Growing Intimacy with the Lord Jesus Christ

Assignments for This Week:

• Listen to chapter 1 in the Audio Guidebook, *People of Promise*.

• Create a memorable moment with Jesus.

• Memorize a verse to help you confess and confront a signature sin.

• Have a friend or family member ask you how you're doing on the promises and action steps.

Daily Assignments:

• Read the assigned Scripture passages and answer the questions.

• Pray the Promises Worth Keeping Prayer.

• Write down your simple acts of servant love (pp. 64–65).

Introduction to Theme 1: Nurture a Growing Intimacy with the Lord Jesus Christ

SUNDAY

Theme 1 runs Sunday through Friday, Days 1–6

Read Luke 10:38-42.   Date_____

You intended to spend some quality time with your parents in their last years. But demands at work and expectations at home made this next to impossible. Now, they're both gone!

Is it like that with Jesus also? He's the one who's done more for you than anyone else. But finding even a few minutes for him in a busy day or month has proved next to impossible.

Would you believe that nurturing a growing intimacy with the Lord doesn't have to be all that intimidating? During these coming 50 days, it translates into interacting with a short scripture each day, making the Promises Worth Keeping Prayer your own, and setting aside seven special quarter hours when, like Mary, you give Jesus your undivided attention.

Maybe you'll choose to write a list of ten great ways he's blessed you, or eight times he's rescued you from trouble. Could you do that?

Sure, you're as busy as Martha. But can you hear Jesus say that Mary chose a better way?

1. What was Martha distracted with during Christ's visit? What did Jesus say about Mary's actions in contrast to Martha's?

_____

_____

_____

2. What distractions in your life might keep you from nurturing a growing intimacy with Jesus?

_____

_____

_____

3. How does Christ's response to the situation help you evaluate your own distractions? Name one specific way you could change your lifestyle to better focus on what is truly important.

_____

_____

_____

Additional Thoughts

_____

_____

_____

_____

_____

_____

_____

_____

_____

_____

_____

_____

_____

_____

_____

_____

_____

DAY 2

Theme 1: Nurture a Growing
Intimacy with the Lord Jesus Christ

Read Psalm 63.   Date_____

1. David was being chased by his enemies through the desert. In one sentence, how would you summarize his attitude toward God in this psalm?

_____

_____

_____

2. List three images David uses to describe his relationship with God. What human longings do these images represent?

_____

_____

_____

3. If you were to write your own psalm with a similar theme, what original images would you choose to show that you long for intimacy with God?

_____

_____

_____

4. Do harsh circumstances tend to push you closer to God or farther away? Explain. Describe a time when, faced with difficult circumstances, you encountered God in a memorable way.

_____

_____

_____

5. One way to pursue spiritual intimacy is to "create memorable moments with Jesus." What are your initial ideas about what you can do this week (see p. 9)?

_____

_____

_____

❑ Pray the Promises Worth Keeping Prayer on page 9.
❑ Write down your simple act of servant love on page 64–65.
❑ Listen to chapter 1 in the *People of Promise* Audio Guidebook.

Additional Thoughts

_____

_____

_____

_____

_____

_____

_____

_____

_____

_____

_____

_____

_____

_____

_____

DAY 3

Theme 1: Nurture a Growing Intimacy with the Lord Jesus Christ

Read Revelation 2:1–7.   Date_____

1. What are the good things Jesus says about the church at Ephesus? If you had been a first-century Ephesian, would you have thought of this as a good, strong church? Why or why not?

_____

_____

_____

2. What was Christ's one criticism of the Ephesian church? What in this passage indicates the seriousness of this fault?

_____

_____

_____

3. When in your life was your relationship with Jesus fresh and meaningful? Describe it.

_____

_____

_____

4. In what ways is your present relationship with Christ similar to and/or different from the time you described?

_____

_____

_____

5. What activities have characteristically helped you draw near to God? How could you incorporate one of them in your "memorable moments with Jesus" (see p. 9) this week?

_____

_____

_____

❑ Pray the Promises Worth Keeping Prayer on page 9.
❑ Write down your simple act of servant love on page 64–65.
❑ Memorize a verse (see *The Little Scripture Pack for Practicing Purity*, duplicated on pp. 121–126).

Additional Thoughts

_____

_____

_____

_____

_____

_____

_____

_____

_____

_____

_____

_____

_____

_____

DAY 4

Theme 1: Nurture a Growing Intimacy with the Lord Jesus Christ

Read 1 John 1:1–10.   **Date_____**

1. God seems impersonal and distant to many people. List several ways John says he encountered Jesus Christ personally (verses 1–2).

_____

_____

_____

2. While we presently do not have the same privileges John did, all believers can have intimacy with Jesus. What will help you live today, remembering this promise of future intimacy (memorize a Bible verse, find a picture of Jesus to carry with you, and so on)?

_____

_____

_____

3. This special intimacy with Jesus has implications about the way we live our lives. Summarize the main point of verses 5–10.

_____

_____

_____

4. Name any attitude or behavior in your life that creates a barrier to your intimacy with Jesus.

_____

_____

_____

5. How do you think Jesus feels when you hurt someone you love? With this in mind, what do you want to tell that person?

_____

_____

_____

❏ Pray the Promises Worth Keeping Prayer on page 9.
❏ Write down your simple act of servant love on pages 64–65.
❏ Listen to chapter 1 in the *People of Promise* Audio Guidebook.

Additional Thoughts

_____

_____

_____

_____

_____

_____

_____

_____

_____

_____

_____

_____

_____

_____

_____

_____

_____

DAY 5

Theme 1: Nurture a Growing Intimacy with the Lord Jesus Christ

Read Mark 1:32–39.   **Date**_____

1. Describe the demands that were being placed on Jesus.

_____

_____

_____

2. How did Jesus react to being in such demand (verse 35)? Why do you think he responded that way?

_____

_____

_____

3. How might your life be improved during busy times if you followed Jesus' example?

_____

_____

_____

4. When is a time this past week when Jesus might have said to you, "Wouldn't you rather spend time with me than _____ (watch TV, talk on the phone, do housework, spend time on the computer, and so on)?"

_____

_____

_____

❑ Pray the Promises Worth Keeping Prayer on page 9.
❑ Write down your simple act of servant love on pages 64–65.
❑ Create a memorable moment with Jesus.

Additional Thoughts

DAY 6

Theme 1: Nurture a Growing Intimacy with the Lord Jesus Christ

Read Psalm 73:25-28.   Date_____

1. What words does the psalmist, Asaph, use to describe his intimate relationship with God? How would you express similar feelings in your own words?

_____

_____

_____

2. Earlier in the psalm, Asaph notes that the ungodly seem to have material wealth and an easy life (verses 2–14). When is a time you've felt like Asaph?

_____

_____

_____

3. Verses 16–24 are the turning point in this psalm. Describe how Asaph's perspective changed after entering the sanctuary of God.

_____

_____

_____

4. All of us would like to experience God's presence in his sanctuary as the psalmist did. As you anticipate the Lord's Day, what are some ways you can better open yourself to this possibility?

_____

_____

_____

5. Asaph discovered that his intimacy with God put him in an enviable position. Rephrase verse 28 in a way that makes it your own.

_____

_____

_____

❑ Pray the Promises Worth Keeping Prayer on page 9.
❑ Write down your simple act of servant love on pages 64–65.
❑ Have a friend or family member ask you how you're doing on the promises and action steps.

Additional Thoughts

_____

_____

_____

_____

_____

_____

_____

_____

_____

_____

_____

_____

_____

_____

Check the box if you have completed the assignment.

❑ Completed Days 1–6.
❑ Prayed the Promises Worth Keeping Prayer.
❑ Wrote down my simple acts of servant love.
❑ Listened to chapter 1 in the *People of Promise* Audio Guidebook.
❑ Memorized a verse.
❑ Created a memorable moment with Jesus.
❑ Had someone ask about my Adventure progress.

Optional Follow-up Scriptures for Extra Study on Theme 1:

2 Peter 1:16–18   Ephesians 3:14–21
Matthew 11:28–30   Isaiah 30:15

MOVING FORWARD

Theme 2: Cultivate Vital Friendships That Encourage Me to Keep My Promises

Assignments for This Week:
• Listen to chapter 2 in the *People of Promise* Audio Guidebook
• Create a memorable moment with Jesus.
• Memorize a verse to help you confess and confront a signature sin.
• Have a friend or family member ask you how you're doing on the promises and action steps.

Daily Assignments:
• Read the assigned Scripture passages and answer the questions.
• Pray the Promises Worth Keeping Prayer.
• Write down your simple acts of servant love (pp. 64–65).

Theme 2 runs Saturday through Friday, Days 7–13

Read Proverbs 27:6, 9, 17.   Date_____

Most things don't stay sharp on their own. Pencils don't. Knives don't. And for the most part, Christians don't. So, this Adventure is a time to discover how valuable another person can be in keeping you spiritually sharp.

Did you know that most Christians find it easier to stay alert when praying with someone else than when praying alone? Discussing Scripture is usually more stimulating than meditating on it alone. Talking over spiritual goals with a friend is often more productive than keeping your plans to yourself.

Like the sweet smell of perfume, a friend's counsel can be extremely pleasant. Are you presently experiencing this? If "wounds from a friend can be trusted," do you know someone well enough to let that person talk honestly about where he or she thinks you are spiritually? That famous proverb reads, "iron sharpens iron." Do you agree?

Again, most things don't stay sharp on their own!

1. When has a friend lovingly confronted you about something, given you sound advice, or helped to sharpen you? How did you benefit from the experience?

_____

_____

_____

2. Name some people who have earned the right to challenge or sharpen you. How might you be a friend to them in the same way?

_____

_____

_____

3. What are three reasons people don't have more of these vital friendships? Which of these barriers is most crucial for you to break through?

_____

_____

_____

Additional Thoughts

_____

_____

_____

_____

_____

_____

_____

_____

_____

_____

_____

_____

_____

_____

_____

Theme 2: Cultivate Vital Friendships
That Encourage Me to Keep My Promises

Read Romans 1:11–12.   Date_____

1. According to these verses, what reasons does Paul give for longing to see the believers at Rome?

_____

_____

_____

2. Does it surprise you to hear that this great apostle needs the church at Rome as much as they need him? Why or why not?

_____

_____

_____

3. If Paul couldn't "go it alone," neither can you. As you "come out of spiritual isolation," what is an area of your life you could be more open to talking about? Have you found someone you could trust with this information? (See Action Step 2, p. 10.)

_____

_____

_____

4. What are needs you have that your small group or community of faith might be able to meet?

_____

_____

_____

5. Paul writes about mutual encouragement. Name one way you can encourage a fellow believer this week.

_____

_____

_____

❑ Pray the Promises Worth Keeping Prayer on page 9.
❑ Write down your simple act of servant love on pages 64–65.
❑ Listen to chapter 2 in the *People of Promise* Audio Guidebook.

Additional Thoughts

_____

_____

_____

_____

_____

_____

_____

_____

_____

_____

_____

_____

_____

_____

TUESDAY

Theme 2: Cultivate Vital Friendships That Encourage Me to Keep My Promises

Read Daniel 1.   Date_____

1. According to the first seven verses, what was Daniel's situation? Describe a similar scenario if the same thing were to happen in today's world.

_____

_____

_____

2. According to verse 8, what was Daniel's response to the king's food and wine?

_____

_____

_____

3. When were you recently tempted to participate in a practice you knew was wrong? How did you respond?

_____

_____

_____

4. In verses 11–16 it is clear that three of Daniel's associates also decided to abstain from the king's provisions. Based on their experiences, how might supportive friendships help you resolve to live what you say you believe?

_____

_____

_____

5. After 10 days, the king saw an observable difference in Daniel and his friends. After 10 days of this Spiritual Adventure, what observable growth have you noticed in your life?

_____

_____

_____

❑ Pray the Promises Worth Keeping Prayer on page 9.
❑ Write down your simple act of servant love on pages 64–65.
❑ Create a memorable moment with Jesus.

Additional Thoughts

_____

_____

_____

_____

_____

_____

_____

_____

_____

_____

_____

_____

Theme 2: Cultivate Vital Friendships
That Encourage Me to Keep My Promises

Read James 5:13–20.   Date_____

1. Identify a fellow Christian who is in trouble (verse 13), happy (verse 13), sick (verse 14), in sin (verse 15), or wandering from the truth (verse 19).

_____

_____

_____

2. Based on the text or your experience, how might being a part of the body of Christ benefit these people?

_____

_____

_____

3. When do you recall the prayers of church people on your behalf being especially meaningful?

_____

_____

_____

4. In verse 16, what two things does James instruct us to do? Assuming James was writing to house churches, how might that setting have made it easier for Christians to carry out these instructions than in present-day churches?

_____

_____

_____

5. Describe several environments that capture the relational dynamic James wrote about that would make it more comfortable for you to share your struggles and pray with others.

_____

_____

_____

❑ Pray the Promises Worth Keeping Prayer on page 9.
❑ Write down your simple act of servant love on pages 64–65.
❑ Listen to chapter 2 in the *People of Promise* Audio Guidebook.

Additional Thoughts

_____

_____

_____

_____

_____

_____

_____

_____

_____

_____

_____

_____

_____

_____

_____

THURSDAY

Theme 2: Cultivate Vital Friendships
That Encourage Me to Keep My Promises

Read 1 Samuel 20:1–17.   **Date**_____

1. This passage provides a powerful picture of the kind of mutual support needed during times of adversity. What clues are given that reveal the strength of the friendship between David and Jonathan?

_____

_____

_____

2. What did David and Jonathan do in verses 16–17? What family dynamics made this significant?

_____

_____

_____

3. Apart from someone in your immediate family, who has been, or is now, a Jonathan in your life? What are some difficult events in which this person was able to support you? How has the relationship been reciprocal?

_____

_____

_____

4. What acquaintances in your life could potentially develop into the type of committed, God-centered friendship that David and Jonathan enjoyed?

_____

_____

_____

5. How is God answering the Promises Worth Keeping Prayer you are praying each day, "Guide me to godly friends who will help me remain pure and honor my priorities"?

_____

_____

_____

❑ Pray the Promises Worth Keeping prayer on page 9.
❑ Write down your simple act of servant love on pages 64–65.
❑ Memorize a verse (see *The Little Scripture Pack for Practicing Purity*, duplicated on pp. 121–126).

Additional Thoughts

_____

_____

_____

_____

_____

_____

_____

_____

_____

_____

_____

_____

_____

_____

_____

_____

_____

Theme 2: Cultivate Vital Friendships
That Encourage Me to Keep My Promises

Read Ecclesiastes 4:9–12.   **Date**_____

1. What general principle is Solomon stating in this passage? What are some everyday examples of this truth?

_____

_____

_____

2. What are the benefits related to friendship that Solomon lists in this passage?

_____

_____

_____

3. How might Solomon's general principle that life is better with a friend's help enhance your spiritual life? Be specific.

_____

_____

_____

4. What new thought does Solomon add with the "cord of three strands"? How does that benefit you more than having just one other friend?

_____

_____

_____

5. Write a two-sentence progress report on how you're doing with Action Step 2—"Come out of spiritual isolation."

_____

_____

_____

❏ Pray the Promises Worth Keeping Prayer on page 9.
❏ Write down your simple act of servant love on pages 64–65.
❏ Have a friend or family member ask you how you're doing on the promises and action steps.

Additional Thoughts

_____

_____

_____

_____

_____

_____

_____

_____

_____

_____

_____

_____

_____

_____

_____

_____

Check the box if you have completed the assignment.
- ❑ Completed Days 7–13.
- ❑ Prayed the Promises Worth Keeping Prayer.
- ❑ Wrote down my simple acts of servant love (pp. 64–65).
- ❑ Listened to chapter 2 in the *People of Promise* Audio Guidebook.
- ❑ Memorized a verse.
- ❑ Created a memorable moment with Jesus.
- ❑ Had someone ask about my Adventure progress.

Optional Follow-up Scriptures for Extra Study on Theme 2:

Galatians 6:1–4   Ephesians 6:21–22
Romans 16:1–16   Mark 6:6–12

Theme 3: Practice Purity in Thought and Action

Assignments for This Week:
- Listen to chapter 3 in the *People of Promise* Audio Guidebook.
- Create a memorable moment with Jesus.
- Memorize a verse to help you confess and confront a signature sin.
- Have a friend or family member ask you how you're doing on the promises and action steps.
- Begin the process of confessing and confronting a signature sin.

Daily Assignments:
- Read the assigned Scripture passages and answer the questions.
- Pray the Promises Worth Keeping Prayer.
- Write down your simple acts of servant love (pp. 64–65).

Theme 3 runs Saturday through Friday, Days 14–20

Read Hebrews 12:1–3.   Date_____

Do you sometimes wonder how people get attracted to certain pets? For example, how do you go for a leisurely walk in the park with a tarantula on the end of your leash, or an alligator, or a Bengal tiger?

Christians get attracted to pet sins as well. But running the race of faith with a six-foot python wrapped around an arm and a leg makes little sense.

In this passage, the stadium is filled with past heroes of the faith. They can hardly be expected to get excited, however, if most of the contemporary Christian runners have handicapped themselves. Only when the entangling coils of the Great Serpent are removed is there the promise of something good happening on the track.

What hinders you from running the way you could if you were at your best for Jesus? During this Adventure, might you be wise to question whether the attraction of a given sin is really all that great?

1. When was the last time you were in a race? Was anyone watching? In verse 1, what are the Hebrew believers instructed to do in their race of faith? Who was cheering them on, and who is cheering you on?

_____

_____

_____

2. Verse 1 suggests the image of casting aside a garment or burden that hinders athletes from running their best. What is a sin that repeatedly trips you up (see discussion of "signature sin," p. 12)?

_____

_____

_____

3. As you fix your eyes on Jesus, what aspect of his life would be particularly helpful in resisting your "signature sin"?

_____

_____

_____

Additional Thoughts

_____

_____

_____

_____

_____

_____

_____

_____

_____

_____

_____

_____

_____

_____

_____

DAY 16

Theme 3: Practice Purity in Thought and Action

Read Genesis 39:1–23.   Date_____

1. According to verses 1–6, why did Joseph prosper? How is Joseph's gratitude to God reflected in verses 8–9?

_____

_____

_____

2. Joseph was young and single in a country far from home. What did Potiphar's wife do to play on his vulnerability (verses 10–12)?

_____

_____

_____

3. Identify a temptation that constantly parades in front of you. Do you tend to repeatedly succumb to this temptation? Why do you think that is?

_____

_____

_____

4. Joseph made changes in his life to purposely avoid temptation. What steps can you take that would benefit you in a similar way? (See Action Step 3 for ideas.)

_____

_____

_____

5. A key to Joseph's success was the constant awareness of God's presence. How can you become more aware that God is with you every moment of every day, whatever you're going through?

_____

_____

_____

❑ Pray the Promises Worth Keeping Prayer on page 9.
❑ Write down your simple act of servant love on pages 64–65.
❑ Listen to chapter 3 in the *People of Promise* Audio Guidebook.

Additional Thoughts

_____

_____

_____

_____

_____

_____

_____

_____

_____

_____

_____

_____

_____

_____

DAY 17

Theme 3: Practice Purity in Thought and Action

Read Romans 6:12–23.   Date_____

1. In verses 12–14, Paul instructs the Roman believers not to do two specific things, but instead to do something else. In your own words, state what the two negative commands are in verses 12 and 13a. What are the Roman believers to do instead (verse 13b)?

_____

_____

_____

2. Paul uses the analogy of slavery to make the point that righteousness, not sin, should be the Christian's master. If an observer were to watch your life for a week, who would that person say is your master? What reasons would be given?

_____

_____

_____

3. Christ's death has set us free from sin. Picture what your life would be like if you were no longer mastered by your "signature sin." List a few of these exciting possibilities.

_____

_____

_____

4. One of the first steps to overcoming a negative, repetitive pattern is to realize the consequences of participating in that sin and the rewards of overcoming it. Reread this passage out loud, substituting your specific "signature sin" (see p. 12) in place of the word *sin* every time it occurs.

_____

_____

_____

❑ Pray the Promises Worth Keeping Prayer on page 9.
❑ Write down your simple act of servant love on pages 64–65.
❑ Create a memorable moment with Jesus.

Additional Thoughts

_____

_____

_____

_____

_____

_____

_____

_____

_____

_____

_____

_____

_____

_____

_____

DAY 18

WEDNESDAY

Theme 3: Practice Purity in Thought and Action

Read Psalm 119:9–16.   Date_____

1. What is the common thread in the psalmist's comments here?

_____

_____

_____

2. Which words in this passage indicate that knowing and obeying Scripture is not a burden?

_____

_____

_____

3. The psalmist rejoiced in God's words as much as one rejoices in getting rich (see verse 14). Recall a time when you found a particular scripture especially valuable. What were your feelings?

_____

_____

_____

4. When tempted by a habitual sin, how many times out of ten are you able to cite an appropriate scripture and resist the temptation? What clues in these verses indicate the steps by which the psalmist was able to hide God's words in his heart?

_____

_____

_____

5. Have you identified a scripture to help you overcome your "signature sin"? What verses in this passage might you consider memorizing?

_____

_____

_____

❑ Pray the Promises Worth Keeping Prayer on page 9.
❑ Write down your simple act of servant love on pages 64–65.
❑ Memorize a verse (see *The Little Scripture Pack for Practicing Purity*, duplicated on pp. 121–126).

Additional Thoughts

_____

_____

_____

_____

_____

_____

_____

_____

_____

_____

_____

_____

_____

_____

Theme 3: Practice Purity in Thought and Action

Read Colossians 3:1–17.   **Date**_____

1. Since this Adventure began, which verses in this passage have more characterized your life, verses 5–9 or 12–17 ?

_____

_____

_____

2. According to verses 1–4 and 9–10, what evidence does Paul give that purity is possible?

_____

_____

_____

3. Based on verses 5–9, choose one "article of clothing" you need to remove from your spiritual wardrobe.

_____

_____

_____

4. It's easy to think of purity simply as getting rid of our old stuff. But Paul talks about a complete makeover. As you take steps to overcome your "signature sin," what thought or action would you like to try on in its place?

_____

_____

_____

❑ Pray the Promises Worth Keeping Prayer on page 9.
❑ Write down your simple act of servant love on pages 64–65.
❑ Have a friend or family member ask you how you're doing on the promises and action steps.

Additional Thoughts

_____

_____

_____

_____

_____

_____

_____

_____

_____

_____

_____

_____

_____

_____

_____

_____

_____

_____

Theme 3: Practice Purity in Thought and Action

Read Philippians 4:8–9.   **Date**_____

1. Where does your mind normally go when doing something that doesn't require your full attention (driving, doing dishes, and so on)?

_____

_____

_____

2. How does what you think about correspond to Paul's words in verse 8? Explain.

_____

_____

_____

3. How does the way you use your discretionary time (TV, reading, conversations, and so forth) feed your thought life?

_____

_____

_____

4. Carefully identify one quality from verse 8 that you would like to mark your thought life. What changes do you need to make for this to develop?

_____

_____

_____

5. You've heard it said, "Practice makes perfect." Since the God of peace is with us in the process, what do you need most from him as you learn to practice purity?

_____

_____

_____

❑ Pray the Promises Worth Keeping Prayer on page 9.
❑ Write down your simple act of servant love on pages 64–65.
❑ Trust God's power to defeat one area of impurity in your life.

Additional Thoughts

_____

_____

_____

_____

_____

_____

_____

_____

_____

_____

_____

_____

_____

_____

_____

Check the box if you have completed the assignment.
- ❑ Completed Days 14–20.
- ❑ Prayed the Promises Worth Keeping Prayer.
- ❑ Wrote down my simple acts of servant love (pp. 64–65).
- ❑ Listened to chapter 3 in the *People of Promise* Audio Guidebook.
- ❑ Memorized a verse.
- ❑ Created a memorable moment with Jesus.
- ❑ Had someone ask about my Adventure progress.
- ❑ Began to confront and confess a signature sin.

Optional Follow-up Scriptures for Extra Study on Theme 3:

Ephesians 5:1–9	Exodus 20:1–17
1 Corinthians 6:9–20	Matthew 5:27–30

MOVING FORWARD ►

Theme 4: Make Family Relationships a Priority

Assignments for This Week:
- Listen to chapter 4 in the *People of Promise* Audio Guidebook.
- Create a memorable moment with Jesus.
- Memorize a verse to help you confess and confront a signature sin.
- Have a friend or family member ask you how you're doing on the promises and action steps.

Daily Assignments:
- Read the assigned Scripture passages and answer the questions.
- Pray the Promises Worth Keeping Prayer.
- Write down your simple acts of servant love (pp. 64–65).

Theme 4 runs Saturday through Friday, Days 21–27

Read Matthew 20:20–28.   Date_____

True or false: Only the wealthy can afford to have servants in their homes.

The statement is true if your thinking about servants is restricted to the way the term is popularly understood. But if your mind grasps what Jesus is saying in this passage, every Christian home can have servants. Beginning with the adults and including all but the youngest of children, everyone in the home should make it a point to lovingly look after the needs of others. After all, isn't that what a servant does?

Maybe you're more adept at lording it over people. Your Lord says this isn't how it's to be done by those who copy his ways. Instead, true greatness is demonstrated by consistently putting others first.

Best of all, having a number of servants of this kind doesn't add a penny to the family budget. What a great and affordable service! Are you taking advantage of it?

1. Although it's natural to want good things for those we love, how did Jesus respond to the request of the mother of James and John?

_____

_____

_____

2. Part of making family relationships a priority is being willing to serve. Jesus is the ultimate example of this type of servanthood (verse 28). When recently have you been served by a family member or friend? How did it affect your relationship with him or her?

_____

_____

_____

Continued on page 66

SIMPLE ACTS OF SERVANT LOVE

In the spaces provided, write down your simple acts of servant love. Each day of the Adventure, do something simple to care for someone you care about. For more information on Action Step 4, Care for Those You Care About, see page 15.

Day 1

Day 2

Day 3

Day 4

Day 5

Day 6

Day 7

Day 8

Day 9

Day 10

Day 11

Day 12

Day 13

Day 14

Day 15

Day 16

Day 17

Day 18

Day 19

Day 20

Day 21

Day 22

Day 23

Day 24

Day 25

Day 26

Day 27

Day 28

Day 29

Day 30

Day 31

Day 32

Day 33

Day 34

Day 35

Day 36

Day 37

Day 38

Day 39

Day 40

Day 41

Day 42

Day 43

Day 44

Day 45

Day 46

Day 47

Day 48

Day 49

Day 50

3. What hinders you from being a better servant to your family? How might you reorder your priorities to care more for those you care about?

_____

_____

_____

Additional Thoughts

_____

_____

_____

_____

_____

_____

_____

_____

_____

_____

_____

_____

_____

_____

_____

Theme 4: Make Family Relationships a Priority

Read Esther 2:5–11.   Date_____

1. What was Mordecai's family relationship with Esther? What action did he take when her parents died?

_____

_____

_____

2. Put yourself in Mordecai's place. What might have been difficult about taking her as his own?

_____

_____

_____

3. Picture one of your extended family members in a difficult situation. How might Mordecai have responded to this relative's need?

_____

_____

_____

4. What in this passage indicates that Mordecai showed an active interest in Esther when she was no longer under his roof? How might you show a similar concern for family members who don't live with you?

_____

_____

_____

5. Action Step 4 is to care for those you care about by doing simple acts of servant love. How might one of those acts this week be directed toward someone outside your nuclear family?

_____

_____

_____

❑ Pray the Promises Worth Keeping Prayer on page 9.
❑ Write down your simple act of servant love on pages 64–65.
❑ Listen to chapter 4 in the *People of Promise* Audio Guidebook.

Additional Thoughts

_____

_____

_____

_____

_____

_____

_____

_____

_____

_____

_____

_____

_____

_____

Theme 4: Make Family Relationships a Priority

Read Ephesians 5:21—6:4.   **Date**_____

1. We often take for granted those we care most about. How does Paul's advice correct this tendency?

_____

_____

_____

2. What part of these instructions would be difficult for you to live up to? Explain.

_____

_____

_____

3. Paul uses the analogy of Christ's relationship to his own body, the church, to illustrate the kind of loving devotion that should characterize husband-and-wife relationships. How is Christlike love observable in your life?

_____

_____

_____

4. How specifically are you challenged by Paul's instructions on parent-child relationships?

_____

_____

_____

5. In an effort to emulate Christ, what simple act of servant love can you do for someone in your immediate family today?

_____

_____

_____

❑ Pray the Promises Worth Keeping Prayer on page 9.
❑ Write down your simple act of servant love on pages 64–65.
❑ Memorize a verse (see *The Little Scripture Pack for Practicing Purity*, duplicated on pp. 121–126).

Additional Thoughts

_____

_____

_____

_____

_____

_____

_____

_____

_____

_____

_____

_____

_____

_____

_____

WEDNESDAY

Theme 4: Make Family Relationships a Priority

Read Genesis 50:15–21.   Date_____

1. What had Joseph's brothers done to him earlier that worried them now that their father had died? (See Genesis 37:12–36 if you are unfamiliar with Joseph's story.) What's the worst thing a loved one has done to you?

_____

_____

_____

2. Based on your responses to those who have wronged you, what are several ways Joseph could have reacted against his brothers?

_____

_____

_____

3. How was Joseph's response different than those you listed above? Why might this seem unrealistic to some?

_____

_____

_____

4. Forgiving those who have hurt us is one of the most difficult challenges in a family. What was Joseph's secret, and how might that relate to your situation?

_____

_____

_____

5. It took the death of their father for Joseph and his brothers to be reconciled. What could you do to safeguard extended family relationships before the loss of a loved one?

_____

_____

_____

❑ Pray the Promises Worth Keeping Prayer on page 9.
❑ Write down your simple act of servant love on pages 64–65.
❑ Create a memorable moment with Jesus.

Additional Thoughts

_____

_____

_____

_____

_____

_____

_____

_____

_____

_____

_____

_____

THURSDAY

Theme 4: Make Family Relationships a Priority

Read Deuteronomy 6:1–9.   Date_____

1. What specific instructions does Moses have for parents in this passage? What benefits does he give?

_____

_____

_____

2. Moses makes reference to three generations. What spiritual foundations were passed down to you from parents and grandparents? What are you doing to lay a spiritual foundation for future generations?

_____

_____

_____

3. One of the assumptions of this passage is that children and parents naturally spend large amounts of time together. What often prevents that from happening today?

_____

_____

_____

4. You can make the most of the time your family *does* have together. Based on Moses' instructions in verses 7–9, what can you do to incorporate Christian elements into normal routines such as mealtime, driving, watching TV, and so on?

_____

_____

_____

5. In order to achieve the above goal, what might you need to sacrifice for the privilege of leaving a spiritual legacy?

_____

_____

_____

❑ Pray the Promises Worth Keeping Prayer on page 9.
❑ Write down your simple act of servant love on pages 64–65.
❑ Continue the process of confessing and confronting a signature sin.

Additional Thoughts

_____

_____

_____

_____

_____

_____

_____

_____

_____

_____

_____

_____

_____

_____

_____

_____

Theme 4: Make Family Relationships a Priority

Read 2 Samuel 9:1–13.   Date_____

1. David promised to show kindness to Jonathan's household (see Day 12). Now, years later, how does David keep his promise?

_____

_____

_____

2. In keeping with his culture, David extends the boundaries of family to include the relatives of his friends. How might caring for your friends include showing concern for their children?

_____

_____

_____

3. David asked if there were anyone to whom he could show kindness. Ask yourself a similar question: Is there anyone in my church family who has a special need (children of the divorced, people with disabilities, single parents, and so on)?

_____

_____

_____

4. Like David, we can invite Mephibosheths to sit at our family table. What practical ways can you welcome others into your life (offering to baby-sit, give tuition support, provide meals for shut-ins, and so forth)?

_____

_____

_____

❑ Pray the Promises Worth Keeping Prayer on page 9.

❑ Write down your simple act of servant love on pages 64–65.

❑ Have a friend or family member ask you how you're doing on the promises and action steps.

Additional Thoughts

Check the box if you have completed the assignment.

- ❑ Completed Days 21–27.
- ❑ Prayed the Promises Worth Keeping Prayer.
- ❑ Wrote down my simple acts of servant love (pp. 64–65).
- ❑ Listened to chapter 4 in the *People of Promise* Audio Guidebook.
- ❑ Memorized a verse.
- ❑ Created a memorable moment with Jesus.
- ❑ Had someone ask about my Adventure progress.
- ❑ Began to confess and confront a signature sin.

Optional Follow-up Scriptures for Extra Study on Theme 4:

Mark 1:29–31   2 Timothy 1:3–7
Exodus 18:1–12   Psalm 68:4–6

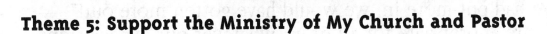

MOVING FORWARD ▶

Theme 5: Support the Ministry of My Church and Pastor

Assignments for This Week:

- Listen to chapter 5 in the *People of Promise* Audio Guidebook.
- Create a memorable moment with Jesus.
- Memorize a verse to help you confess and confront a signature sin.
- Have a friend or family member ask how you're doing on the promises and action steps.

Daily Assignments:

- Read the assigned Scripture passages and answer the questions.
- Pray the Promises Worth Keeping Prayer.
- Write down your simple acts of servant love (pp. 64–65).

Theme 5 runs Saturday through Friday, Days 28—34

Read Ephesians 4:1—7, 11—16.   Date_____

In pioneer days, churches were often served by circuit-riding preachers. On one such trip, a minister's ten-year-old son rode horseback with him. As they came to the first of several log sanctuaries, the father/son team put three coins in the offering box at the back. Though the meeting was attended by just a handful, it was this pastor's privilege to take what was left in the offering box as payment for services rendered.

The inexperienced son watched as his expectant father turned the box over and emptied out . . . the same few coins they had given earlier. Attempting to be helpful, the young boy told his disappointed father, "If we had put more in, we would have gotten more out!"

His words are appropriate for all of us, whatever our expectations regarding the church. The degree to which we are truly supportive often determines how much we receive from our church and pastor.

1. In this passage, what is the role of the pastoral staff in the church? What is the role of every individual in the congregation?

_____

_____

_____

2. You're more essential to the health or well-being of your church than you might think. What is something you do well? How might your talents or skills be helpful to your church or pastor?

_____

_____

_____

3. If your church went in for a complete physical, would your part of the body be diagnosed as being in good shape, needing more exercise, or suffering from overuse? Explain.

_____

_____

_____

Additional Thoughts

_____

_____

_____

_____

_____

_____

_____

_____

_____

_____

_____

_____

_____

_____

_____

DAY 30

Theme 5: Support the Ministry of My Church and Pastor

Read 1 Thessalonians 5:12–13.   **Date**_____

1. What are the three requests Paul makes of the Thessalonians in these verses?

_____

_____

_____

2. On a scale of 1 to 10 (10 being perfect), how do your attitudes and actions toward the spiritual leadership of your church match with Paul's requests? Explain.

_____

_____

_____

3. Paul didn't offer any escape clauses for acting in love toward church leaders. When are you tempted to look for some?

_____

_____

_____

4. Think of a few simple acts of servant love you could do to show respect and esteem for your pastor and church leaders. Look for an opportunity to carry out one of these acts. (A good time might be when you're looking for an escape clause.)

_____

_____

_____

❏ Pray the Promises Worth Keeping Prayer on page 9.
❏ Write down your simple act of servant love on pages 64–65.
❏ Listen to chapter 5 in the *People of Promise* Audio Guidebook.

Additional Thoughts

_____

_____

_____

_____

_____

_____

_____

_____

_____

_____

_____

_____

_____

_____

_____

_____

_____

DAY 31

Theme 5: Support the Ministry of My Church and Pastor

Read Ephesians 6:18–20.   **Date**_____

1. In verse 18 Paul offers a succinct account of how we should pray. List at least three characteristics of prayer from this verse.

_____

_____

_____

2. Paul kept his ministry focus despite imprisonment. What difficulties might today's ministers face that could blur their focus?

_____

_____

_____

3. How often do you pray for the ministry of your church and pastor? Who is someone you might learn from in this regard?

_____

_____

_____

4. Paul states his overriding desire to make known the mystery of the gospel. What smaller issues might be taking your focus off this broader mission of the church?

_____

_____

_____

5. Identify some current needs of your church and pastor, and spend some time praying for them.

_____

_____

_____

❑ Pray the Promises Worth Keeping Prayer on page 9.
❑ Write down your simple act of servant love on page 64–65.
❑ Memorize a verse (see *The Little Scripture Pack for Practicing Purity,* duplicated on pp.121–126).

Additional Thoughts

Theme 5: Support the Ministry of My Church and Pastor

Read Hebrews 10:19–25.   Date_____

1. In verses 19–21 the author gives us the basis for what he asks us to do in verses 22–25. Identify the two reasons given in verses 19–21.

_____

_____

_____

2. Now identify what we are to do in verses 22–25, based on Christ's work.

_____

_____

_____

3. What conclusions would an observer make about the importance you place on church involvement?

_____

_____

_____

4. What benefits do you derive from regular church attendance? How does your presence benefit others?

_____

_____

_____

5. One of the easiest ways to support your church and pastor is by just showing up. Do you need to make any adjustments in your attendance pattern? If so, what are they?

_____

_____

_____

❑ Pray the Promises Worth Keeping Prayer on page 9.
❑ Write down your simple act of servant love on pages 64–65.
❑ Create a memorable moment with Jesus.

Additional Thoughts

Theme 5: Support the Ministry of My Church and Pastor

Read Exodus 35:20—29; 36:2—7.   **Date**_____

1. What was the motivation of the Israelites as they contributed to the construction of the tabernacle? What were the various skills and gifts they offered? (Skim Exodus 35:30—36:1 for more ideas.)

_____

_____

_____

2. What clues are there that these people gave generously? How do you picture the atmosphere and the expression on the faces of the people who invested in this project?

_____

_____

_____

3. Does it surprise you to see the kinds of talents and resources mentioned in this passage? Explain.

_____

_____

_____

4. What is a ministry in your church you're excited about, or you would like to see developed? Who can you talk to about creatively using your gifts in that ministry?

_____

_____

_____

5. If the way you contribute and participate in your church were the standard everyone else followed, would the pastor, like Moses, say there was "more than enough" (see Exodus 36:7)? Why or why not?

_____

_____

_____

❑ Pray the Promises Worth Keeping Prayer on page 9.
❑ Write down your simple act of servant love on pages 64–65.
❑ Continue the process of confessing and confronting a signature sin.

Additional Thoughts

_____

_____

_____

_____

_____

_____

_____

_____

_____

_____

_____

_____

_____

Theme 5: Support the Ministry of My Church and Pastor

Read 2 Corinthians 8:1–9.   Date_____

1. Describe the situation in which the Macedonian churches found themselves. What is intriguing to you about their response?

_____

_____

_____

2. What is a financial trial you've experienced? In what ways does it help you better understand this passage?

_____

_____

_____

3. How would you evaluate your present financial giving? Ask yourself: How often do I give to my church? What is my attitude when I give (see 2 Corinthians 9:6–7)? When is the last time I refrained from buying a nonessential item so I could give to those with more pressing needs?

_____

_____

_____

4. If someone were to pick up your checkbook, what clues would there be that you're a generous Christian? What else might that person learn?

_____

_____

_____

❑ Pray the Promises Worth Keeping Prayer on page 9.
❑ Write down your simple act of servant love on pages 64–65.
❑ Have a friend or family member ask you how you're doing on the promises and action steps.

Additional Thoughts

_____

_____

_____

_____

_____

_____

_____

_____

_____

_____

_____

_____

_____

_____

_____

_____

_____

_____

_____

_____

Check the box if you have completed the assignment.

❑ Completed Days 28–34.
❑ Prayed the Promises Worth Keeping Prayer.
❑ Wrote down my simple acts of servant love (pp. 64–65).
❑ Listened to chapter 5 in the *People of Promise* Audio Guidebook.
❑ Memorized a verse.
❑ Created a memorable moment with Jesus.
❑ Had someone ask about my Adventure progress.
❑ Began to confess and confront a signature sin.

Optional Follow-up Scriptures for Extra Study on Theme 5:

Hebrews 13:15–18   2 Timothy 4:9–18
1 Timothy 5:17–19   Romans 15:30–33

MOVING FORWARD

Theme 6: Identify and Address the Hidden Prejudices of My Heart

Assignments for This Week:
• Listen to chapter 6 in the *People of Promise* Audio Guidebook.
• Create a memorable moment with Jesus.
• Memorize a verse to help you confess and confront a signature sin.
• Have a friend or family member ask you how you're doing on the promises and action steps.
• Choose to become exposed to the suffering of others.

Daily Assignments:
• Read the assigned Scripture passages and answer the questions.
• Pray the Promises Worth Keeping Prayer.
• Write down your simple acts of servant love (pp. 64–65).

Theme 6 runs Saturday through Friday, Days 35–41

Read Luke 10:25–37.   Date_____

It's easy to recognize prejudice when acts of violence are involved. Racial slurs are another obvious evidence of this ugly sin. But it's naive for Christians to think this deep-seated issue has been personally resolved simply because they disassociate themselves from actions of Ku Klux Klan members or neo-Nazis.

All too often it's prejudice that prompts people to look the other way or even to purposely go out of their way so as not to have to confront the suffering of people. Like the two religious leaders in this parable, many contemporary Christians have become adept at thinking that the pain of strangers is something they shouldn't have to deal with. Just avoid those neighborhoods where drugs or guns or prostitution are evident.

On the other hand, who isn't moved by the surprising compassion shown by all Good Samaritans? These Christlike individuals still put themselves at risk to serve those whose troubles they personally had little or nothing to do with.

1. The priest and Levite were religious leaders in positions to offer assistance to the injured man. Samaritans were considered sworn enemies of all Jews. Why do you think Jesus cast the characters the way he did?

_____

_____

_____

2. Wounded travelers in our society are not always so obvious. Who might you have "passed by on the other side of the road"?

_____

_____

3. The Samaritan offers us a good model of how to be a true neighbor by being concerned about the suffering of people we sometimes overlook. To become more exposed to the suffering of others, review Action Step 5 on page 18.

_____

_____

_____

Additional Thoughts

_____

_____

_____

_____

_____

_____

_____

_____

_____

_____

_____

_____

_____

_____

_____

_____

_____

MONDAY

Theme 6: Identify and Address the Hidden Prejudices of My Heart

Read Mark 1:40–42.   Date_____

1. In Jesus' day, lepers were considered outcasts and rejected almost universally because of their disease. Who do you think are modern-day lepers or outcasts?

_____

_____

_____

2. Jewish laws forbade any contact with "the unclean." What was Jesus' emotional and physical response to the man's affliction? What do you suppose Jesus' followers thought about his unexpected response?

_____

_____

_____

3. Clearly Jesus had a place of tenderness for all those with physical afflictions, including lepers. When have you recently followed Jesus' example by showing compassion to someone suffering physically?

_____

_____

_____

4. In Jesus' encounters with people, he saw more than their outward condition. When are you good at getting past outward appearances? When is it more of a struggle?

_____

_____

_____

5. One key to identifying and addressing hidden prejudices is to ask, "Do I see this person, beyond anything else, as God's unique and precious creation?" Write a brief prayer confessing how you have failed to appreciate a modern-day leper as someone made in God's image.

_____

_____

_____

❑ Pray the Promises Worth Keeping Prayer on page 9.
❑ Write down your simple act of servant love on pages 64–65.
❑ Listen to chapter 6 in the *People of Promise* Audio Guidebook.

Additional Thoughts

_____

_____

_____

_____

_____

_____

_____

_____

_____

_____

_____

_____

_____

Theme 6: Identify and Address
the Hidden Prejudices of My Heart

Read John 4:1–42.   Date_____

1. In this passage Jesus was crossing religious, ethnic, and gender "boundaries." To what end did he take that risk (see verses 13, 21–26, 39–42)?

_____

_____

_____

2. Jesus intentionally went through Samaria, a place other Jews wouldn't even set foot in. What geographical boundaries do you not cross to avoid contact with certain kinds of people?

_____

_____

_____

3. Verse 27 states that Jesus' disciples were caught off-guard when they found him talking with a woman. How might that have been a hidden prejudice in their lives?

_____

_____

_____

4. What "boundaries" do you have a hard time crossing when it comes to people who are not from your own background (different denominations, ethnic groups, and so on)?

_____

_____

_____

5. Next time you encounter someone outside your boundaries, picture Jesus right there with you. What could you learn from what he might do?

_____

_____

_____

❏ Pray the Promises Worth Keeping Prayer on page 9.
❏ Write down your simple act of servant love on pages 64–65.
❏ Memorize a verse (see *The Little Scripture Pack for Practicing Purity*, duplicated on pp. 121–126).

Additional Thoughts

_____

_____

_____

_____

_____

_____

_____

_____

_____

_____

_____

_____

_____

Theme 6: Identify and Address
the Hidden Prejudices of My Heart

Read Mark 9:33–41. Date_____

1. What was the subject of the disciples' argument? What was Jesus' response?

_____

_____

_____

2. How can our concern over "who is the greatest" distort our perception of others?

_____

_____

_____

3. Jesus told the disciples to welcome children, who would have been considered among the least of people in his day. What do you do at church to show that you welcome children, that you do not have a hidden prejudice toward them?

_____

_____

_____

4. Another hidden prejudice comes out in verses 38–41. What was Jesus' response concerning someone ministering outside their circle?

_____

_____

_____

5. Think about people ministering in Jesus' name who are not part of your group. How would Jesus respond to your attitude toward them?

_____

_____

_____

❏ Pray the Promises Worth Keeping Prayer on page 9.
❏ Write down your simple act of servant love on pages 64–65.
❏ Create a memorable moment with Jesus.

Additional Thoughts

_____

_____

_____

_____

_____

_____

_____

_____

_____

_____

_____

_____

_____

_____

_____

_____

Theme 6: Identify and Address the Hidden Prejudices of My Heart

Read Matthew 25:31–46.   Date_____

1. Jesus makes it clear that our current actions have future implications. As followers of Christ, what is our present obligation toward others in the world?

_____

_____

_____

2. List some modern-day people with needs similar to those listed in verses 35–36. Do you tend to avoid individuals in these categories? If so, what do your feelings tell you about possible prejudices?

_____

_____

_____

3. According to these verses, how does our service toward others relate to our service to God?

_____

_____

_____

4. What changes might you want to make in your lifestyle to become exposed to the suffering of others?

_____

_____

_____

- ❏ Pray the Promises Worth Keeping Prayer on page 9.
- ❏ Write down your simple act of servant love on pages 64–65.
- ❏ Find a way to become exposed to the suffering of others.

Additional Thoughts

FRIDAY

Theme 6: Identify and Address
the Hidden Prejudices of My Heart

Read Psalm 19:12–14.   Date_____

1. What two different types of sin does David ask forgiveness for and protection from in verses 12–13? How is this inward and outward distinction reinforced in David's requests in verse 14?

_____

_____

_____

2. Which do you have a harder time controlling, your inner thoughts and hidden faults, or your outer speech and actions? What effect does that have on prejudices in your life?

_____

_____

_____

3. As David confronted his hidden faults and prejudices, he became aware of God's strength and grace. In keeping your promise to move beyond prejudices, where do you most need God's rock-solid help?

_____

_____

_____

4. Personalize these verses in a written prayer, confessing the prejudices you've begun to uncover this week and incorporating your answer to Question 3.

_____

_____

_____

- ❑ Pray the Promises Worth Keeping Prayer on page 9.
- ❑ Write down your simple act of servant love on pages 64–65.
- ❑ Have a friend or family member ask you how you're doing on the promises and action steps.
- ❑ Continue to confront your signature sin.

Additional Thoughts

_____

_____

_____

_____

_____

_____

_____

_____

_____

_____

_____

_____

_____

_____

_____

_____

Check the box if you have completed the assignment.

❑ Completed Days 35–41.
❑ Prayed the Promises Worth Keeping Prayer.
❑ Wrote down my simple acts of servant love (pp. 64–65).
❑ Listened to chapter 6 in the *People of Promise* Audio Guidebook.
❑ Memorized a verse.
❑ Created a memorable moment with Jesus.
❑ Had someone ask about my Adventure progress.
❑ Began to confess and confront a signature sin.
❑ Found a way to become exposed to the suffering of others.

Optional Follow-up Scriptures for Extra Study on Theme 6:
Matthew 7:1–5   Ephesians 2:11–18   Psalm 139:23–24

MOVING FORWARD

Theme 7: Influence My World with the Love of Christ
Theme 8: Live One Day at a Time Through the Power of the Risen Christ

Assignments for This Week:
• Listen to chapters 7–8 in the *People of Promise* Audio Guidebook.
• Create a memorable moment with Jesus.
• Memorize a verse to help you confess and confront a signature sin.
• Have a friend or family member ask you how you're doing on the promises and action steps.

Before the Adventure Is Over:
• Identify a "signature sin" and trust God's power to defeat it.
• Find a way to become exposed to the suffering of others.

Daily Assignments:
• Read the assigned Scripture passages and answer the questions.
• Pray the Promises Worth Keeping Prayer.
• Write down your simple acts of servant love (pp. 64–65).

Theme 7 runs Saturday through Thursday, Days 42–47

Read Matthew 28:16–20;   Date_____
Mark 12:28–31.

What do you call someone who claims to be a follower of Jesus but shows little interest in helping others get to know him? This person finds the subject of missions boring, seldom invites anyone to church, and never talks openly about faith in Christ. "My feelings about the Great Commission? If it's all the same to you, Reverend, to keep my interest you need to choose another text."

One of the most forceful preachers America ever produced was Charles Finney (1792—1875). A lawyer by training, time and again the Lord used this Presbyterian to fan the flames of revival throughout the States. Never one to beat around the bush, Finney called such individuals backsliders. Do you agree?

If Finney was right, what does this say about you? Whatever the case, be sure to take Adventure promise #7 seriously about influencing your world with the love of Christ.

1. How does each passage indicate how we are to influence our world with the love of Christ?

_____

_____

_____

2. The original Greek in the Matthew text focuses on making disciples "wherever you go." As you go about your weekly routines, what people make up your world?

_____

_____

_____

3. Choose one person from those you listed whom you could influence for Christ. How can you express God's love to that individual this week?

_____

_____

_____

Additional Thoughts

_____

_____

_____

_____

_____

_____

_____

_____

_____

_____

_____

_____

_____

_____

_____

_____

DAY 44

Theme 7: Influence My World with the Love of Christ

Read Acts 8:26–35.   **Date_____**

1. Philip was never given a reason for setting out on this journey or approaching the Ethiopian (verses 26, 29). How would you describe his response to the divine promptings he received? What was the result?

_____

_____

_____

2. Without explanation, Philip was asked to leave a successful ministry to go to a barren desert setting. When have you sensed the Spirit nudging you to do something that at first didn't make sense? What happened?

_____

_____

_____

3. In response to the Spirit's voice, Philip unexpectedly encountered the Ethiopian. Who is someone who has crossed your path lately? Why might God have brought that person your way?

_____

_____

_____

4. Philip asked a question to discern the Ethiopian's interests and needs. What questions could you ask the person you thought of to begin a friendship for Jesus' sake?

_____

_____

_____

5. Philip and the Ethiopian were from different countries. What's one step you could take to become sensitive to the needs of people different from you (correspond with a missionary, go on a short-term missions trip, befriend an international student, and so forth)?

_____

_____

_____

❑ Pray the Promises Worth Keeping Prayer on page 9.
❑ Write down your simple act of servant love on page 64–65.
❑ Listen to chapter 7 in the *People of Promise* Audio Guidebook.

Additional Thoughts

_____

_____

_____

_____

_____

_____

_____

_____

_____

_____

_____

_____

_____

_____

DAY 45

Theme 7: Influence My World with the Love of Christ

Read Matthew 5:13–16.   Date_____

1. What does Jesus compare his followers with in these verses? Do you think these images are still appropriate today? Why or why not?

_____

_____

_____

2. According to verse 16, why are believers to lead such distinctive lifestyles?

_____

_____

_____

3. In what situations is it difficult for you to be salt and light? Why?

_____

_____

_____

4. When is it easier to let your light shine? Why?

_____

_____

_____

5. What are some examples of what it might mean for you to be salt and light in your world?

_____

_____

_____

❏ Pray the Promises Worth Keeping Prayer on page 9.
❏ Write down your simple act of servant love on page 64–65.
❏ Memorize a verse (see *The Little Scripture Pack for Practicing Purity*, duplicated on pp. 121–126).

Additional Thoughts

_____

_____

_____

_____

_____

_____

_____

_____

_____

_____

_____

_____

_____

_____

_____

_____

_____

_____

DAY 46

Theme 7: Influence My World with the Love of Christ

Read Matthew 9:35–38.   **Date_____**

1. In what three ways was Jesus ministering among the people (verse 35)?

_____

_____

_____

2. Having regularly been in such personal contact with the crowds, what was his "gut reaction" to their plight? According to verse 36, what caused this strong emotional response?

_____

_____

_____

3. Around the world today, who would Jesus see as "harassed and helpless, like sheep without a shepherd"? How is your church showing compassion to some of these groups of people?

_____

_____

_____

4. Jesus was touched when he saw hurting people. Ask the Lord to use this week's national and world news headlines to give you a heart of compassion. Take note of his specific promptings.

_____

_____

_____

❑ Pray the Promises Worth Keeping Prayer on page 9.
❑ Write down your simple act of servant love on page 64–65.
❑ Create a memorable moment with Jesus.

Additional Thoughts

_____
_____
_____
_____
_____
_____
_____
_____
_____
_____
_____
_____
_____
_____
_____
_____
_____
_____
_____
_____
_____
_____
_____

Theme 7: Influence My World with the Love of Christ

Read 2 Corinthians 5:14–21.   Date_____

1. Christ's death is the ultimate demonstration of God's love. What should his love motivate us to do (verses 14–15)?

_____

_____

_____

2. How does Paul say we are not to view others (verse 16)? What do you think that means?

_____

_____

_____

3. How should the perspective of being a new creation in Christ change the way you approach people?

_____

_____

_____

4. Paul points out that God desires to reach his world through us, as his ambassadors. What are some words you associate with that role?

_____

_____

_____

5. As you think of representing Christ as his ambassador, how might that play out at work, in your neighborhood, and so on?

_____

_____

_____

❑ Pray the Promises Worth Keeping Prayer on page 9.
❑ Write down your simple act of servant love on page 64-65.
❑ Have a friend or family member ask you how you're doing on the promises and action steps.

Additional Thoughts

_____
_____
_____
_____
_____
_____
_____
_____
_____
_____
_____
_____
_____
_____
_____
_____
_____
_____
_____
_____

DAY 48

Introduction to Theme 8:
Live One Day at a Time Through
the Power of the Risen Christ

FRIDAY

Theme 8 runs Friday through Sunday, Days 48–50

Read 2 Corinthians 4:7–18.   **Date**_____

Bungee-jumping off a bridge could presumably be called an adventure. But these seven Adventure weeks should have been characterized by more than a rush of spiritual adrenaline.

It's true, Paul had a pump-your-blood experience on the road to Damascus. But as time passed, his life was also marked by a faith lived out daily in spite of major hardships. This passage underscores his resolve not to lose heart, but instead, to be renewed in Christ day by day.

This Adventure is subtitled "Resolving to Live What We Say We Believe." Basic spiritual disciplines have been practiced to help us do this. You're probably not at the level of Christianity Paul practiced, but you've made definite progress. How can you make sure that next Monday through Sunday won't be a time of falling off a bridge? What should you continue resolving to do one day at a time through the power of the resurrected Christ?

1. Paul carried around in his body the death of Jesus (verse 10). In verses 7–12, what specific examples of suffering does he give?

_____

_____

_____

2. In verses 13–15, what hope sustained Paul?

_____

_____

_____

3. As you seek to live one day at a time through the power of the risen Christ, what is one area where you struggle? What encouragement can you draw from verses 16–18?

_____

_____

_____

Additional Thoughts

_____

_____

_____

_____

_____

_____

_____

_____

_____

_____

_____

_____

_____

_____

DAY 49

Theme 8: Live One Day at a Time
Through the Power of the Risen Christ

Read Philippians 3:10–16.   **Date**_____

1. According to these verses, what does Paul want more than anything else in the world (verses 10–11, 14)? In what ways are your desires similar to or different from Paul's?

_____

_____

_____

2. In verses 12–14 Paul uses the image of a runner to describe spiritual growth. In verses 13–14, what does Paul say he does to make progress toward his goal?

_____

_____

_____

3. What are some areas in your life in which you have not "already obtained all this"? What progress have you observed over the past seven weeks?

_____

_____

_____

4. Based on this passage, what would you conclude about the time frame of spiritual growth? What might Coach Paul say to you about maintaining the momentum you have built up during this Adventure?

_____

_____

_____

- ❑ Pray the Promises Worth Keeping Prayer on page 9.
- ❑ Write down your simple act of servant love on page 64–65.
- ❑ Listen to chapter 8 in the *People of Promise* Audio Guidebook.

Additional Thoughts

Theme 8: Live One Day at a Time
Through the Power of the Risen Christ

Read Luke 24:1–12.   Date_____

1. If you were making a movie about the events of the first Easter, how would you direct the actors playing the angels and the women? What type of facial expressions should they have? What should be the tone of their voices? What textual support do you see?

_____

_____

_____

2. What might all of Jesus' followers have done differently that first Easter if they had remembered his promise in verses 6–7?

_____

_____

_____

3. Remembering God's promises helps us live what we say we believe one day at a time. What good habits have you developed during this Adventure that enable you to remember God's words?

_____

_____

_____

4. Peter went away wondering to himself what had happened at the tomb (verse 12). Spend some time reflecting on how the resurrected Christ has used this Adventure to bring about change in your life.

_____

_____

_____

5. Focus your hopes for the days to come in a three-sentence prayer. Thank God for the power you have through the risen Christ.

_____

_____

_____

❑ Pray the Promises Worth Keeping Prayer on page 9.
❑ Write down your simple act of servant love on pages 64–65. Do you have 50 entries?
❑ Complete page 127 to bring closure to your Adventure.
❑ Share your Adventure experience with Mainstay Church Resources and receive a free gift. (See page 128.)

Additional Thoughts

_____

_____

_____

_____

_____

_____

_____

_____

_____

_____

_____

_____

_____

Check the box if you have completed the assignment.

❑ I have completed most of Days 1–50.
❑ I have prayed the Promises Worth Keeping Prayer.
❑ I've recorded my simple acts of servant love.
❑ I've listened to the *People of Promise* Audio Guidebook.
❑ I've set aside time to create memorable moments with Jesus.
❑ I have memorized Bible verses.
❑ I have had a friend or family member ask me how I'm doing on the promises and action steps.
❑ I have identified a "signature sin" in my life and trusted God's power to defeat it.
❑ I have found a way to become exposed to the suffering of others.

Optional Follow-up Scriptures for Extra Study on Themes 7 and 8:
Acts 9:36–42   1 Peter 1:3–9   Acts 2:29–33

MOVING FORWARD

Suggestions:
• Continue to read Scripture and pray daily.
• Seek opportunities to provide simple acts of servant love.
• Keep setting aside special times with Jesus.
• Keep trusting God's power to defeat impurity in your life.
• Look for ways to become exposed to the suffering of others.
• Ask a friend or family member to check regularly on your progress in keeping your promises.

THE LITTLE SCRIPTURE PACK FOR PRACTICING PURITY

The Promises Worth Keeping Prayer

Lord, I want a growing relationship with you. I'm tired of broken promises. Guide me to godly friends who will help me remain pure and honor my priorities. Open my eyes to hidden prejudices in my life. Open my heart to the needs of my church and its leaders. Teach me to reflect your love in the world around me. Help me to _____ so I can live today what I say I believe. Amen.

PURITY Acronym

Put your name by a signature sin.

Unmask who you are before God.

Replace old patterns with new possibilities.

Identify scriptures that keep you focused.

Trust a friend to help you.

Yell for joy whenever you get it right.

May the words of my mouth and the meditation of my heart be pleasing in your sight, O Lord, my Rock and my Redeemer.

(Psalm 19:14, NIV)

But remember that the temptations that come into your life are no different from what others experience. And God is faithful. He will keep the temptation from becoming so strong that you can't stand up against it. When you are tempted, he will show you a way out so that you will not give in to it.

(1 Corinthians 10:13, NLT)

Keep yourselves from sexual promiscuity. Learn to appreciate and give dignity to your body, not abusing it, as is so common among those who know nothing of God.

(1 Thessalonians 4:3b−5, The Message)

Let us behave decently, as in the daytime, not in orgies and drunkenness, not in sexual immorality and debauchery, not in dissension and jealousy. Rather, clothe yourselves with the Lord Jesus Christ, and do not think about how to gratify the desires of the sinful nature.

(Romans 13:13−14, NIV)

How can a young person stay pure? By obeying your word and following its rules . . . . I have hidden your word in my heart, that I might not sin against you.

(Psalm 119:9, 11, NLT)

Therefore, since we are surrounded by such a great cloud of witnesses, let us throw off everything that hinders and the sin that so easily entangles, and let us run with perseverance the race marked out for us. Let us fix our eyes on Jesus, the author and perfecter of our faith, who for the joy set before him endured the cross, scorning its shame, and sat down at the right hand of the throne of God.

(Hebrews 12:1–2, NIV)

And now, dear friends, let me say one more thing as I close this letter. Fix your thoughts on what is true and honorable and right. Think about things that are pure and lovely and admirable. Think about things that are excellent and worthy of praise.

(Philippians 4:8, NLT)

Do not offer the parts of your body to sin, as instruments of wickedness, but rather offer yourselves to God, as those who have been brought from death to life; and offer the parts of your body to him as instruments of righteousness.

(Romans 6:13, NIV)

So, chosen by God for this new life of love, dress in the wardrobe God picked out for you: compassion, kindness, humility, quiet strength, discipline.

(Colossians 3:12, The Message)

Search me, O God, and know my heart: try me, and know my thoughts: And see if there be any wicked way in me, and lead me in the way everlasting.

(Psalm 139:23–24, KJV)

Jesus called the crowd to him and said, "Listen and understand. What goes into a man's mouth does not make him 'unclean,' but what comes out of his mouth, that is what makes him 'unclean.'"

(Matthew 15:10–11, NIV)

Run away from sexual sin! No other sin so clearly affects the body as this one does. For sexual immorality is a sin against your own body. Or don't you know that your body is the temple of the Holy Spirit, who lives in you and was given to you by God? You do not belong to yourself, for God bought you with a high price. So you must honor God with your body.

(1 Corinthians 6:18–20, NLT)

For we have not an high priest which cannot be touched with the feeling of our infirmities; but was in all points tempted like as we are, yet without sin. Let us therefore come boldly unto the throne of grace, that we may obtain mercy, and find grace to help in time of need.

(Hebrews 4:15–16, KJV)

I made a covenant with my eyes not to look with lust upon a young woman.

(Job 31:1, NLT)

Stop loving this evil world and all that it offers you, for when you love the world, you show that you do not have the love of the Father in you. For the world offers only the lust for physical pleasure, the lust for everything we see, and pride in our possessions. These are not from the Father. They are from this evil world.

(1 John 2:15–16, NLT)

Don't keep looking at my sins. Remove the stain of my guilt. Create in me a clean heart, O God. Renew a right spirit within me.

(Psalm 51:9–10, NLT)

"Blessed are those who hunger and thirst for righteousness, for they will be filled. Blessed are the merciful, for they will be shown mercy. Blessed are the pure in heart, for they will see God."

(Matthew 5:6–8, NIV)

Finally, be strong in the Lord and in his mighty power. Put on the full armor of God so that you can take your stand against the devil's schemes.

(Ephesians 6:10–11, NIV)

Love is patient and kind. Love is not jealous or boastful or proud or rude. Love does not demand its own way. Love is not irritable, and it keeps no record of when it has been wronged.

(1 Corinthians 13:4–5, NLT)

Be careful! Watch out for attacks from the Devil, your great enemy. He prowls around like a roaring lion, looking for some victim to devour. Take a firm stand against him, and be strong in your faith.

(1 Peter 5:8–9a, NLT)

Teach me your way, O Lord, and I will walk in your truth; give me an undivided heart, that I may fear your name. I will praise you, O Lord my God, with all my heart; I will glorify your name forever. For great is your love toward me; you have delivered me from the depths of the grave.

(Psalm 86:11–13, NIV)

For where you have envy and selfish ambition, there you find disorder and every evil practice. But the wisdom that comes from heaven is first of all pure; then peace-loving, considerate, submissive, full of mercy and good fruit, impartial and sincere.

(James 3:16–17, NIV)

WE WANT TO HEAR FROM YOU!

Your feedback helps us evaluate the effectiveness of the Spiritual Adventure. Please fill out this comment form and tell us what God did in your life, your church, or your small group during this 50-Day journey. In return for your feedback, we'd like to say thanks by sending you a set of free resources (shown on the next page).

Tell us a story or a specific example of how this Adventure has changed your life or the life of your church or small group.

_____

_____

_____

_____

How can we improve the 50-Day Adventure for you?

_____

_____

_____

_____

How were you involved in the 50-Day Adventure? (Check all that apply.)

❑ Individual   ❑ Entire church

❑ Family   ❑ Small group

❑ Weekend class   ❑ Other

**FOR YOUR FREE THANK-YOU GIFT,
TURN TO THE NEXT PAGE.**

HOW TO GET YOUR FREE GIFTS AND CATALOG!

To say thanks for your feedback, we'll send you a set of five attractive full-color bookmarks with quotations on revival, a 50-Day Spiritual Adventure magnet for your fridge, and your choice of two of the following Little Scripture Packs which make wonderful gifts for those you love. Also, we'll send you our free catalog of resources for building healthy spiritual habits.

Choose from seven Little Scripture Packs (check two):

❑ The Tapped-Out Christian's Little Energy Pack
❑ The Make It Happen Little Scripture Pack for the Church You've Always Longed For
❑ The Believe It or Not Little Scripture Pack for Trusting Christ When Life Gets Confusing
❑ The Overcome Your Fears Little Scripture Pack for Finding Courage When Anxiety Grips Your Heart
❑ The Husband's Little Scripture Pack for Marriage and Family Enrichment
❑ The Wife's Little Scripture Pack for Marriage and Family Enrichment
❑ The Parent's Little Scripture Pack for Parenting and Family Enrichment

Name _____

Street Address _____City_____

State/Prov_____ Zip/Code _____ Phone (___)_____

Church Name _____

Radio station on which you hear "Spiritual Adventure"_____

Mail this order form and evaluation to:

Mainstay Church Resources, Box 30, Wheaton, IL 60189-0030
In Canada: The Chapel Ministries, Box 2000, Waterdown, ON L0R 2H0
or e-mail us your comments at: T50DSA@AOL.com

MO8LFBC99